SandCastle

Word Families Set 7

-ow as in crow

Kelly Doudna

Consulting Editor Monica Marx, M.A./Reading Specialist

ABDO
Publishing Company

Published by SandCastle™, an imprint of ABDO Publishing Company, 4940 Viking Drive, Edina, Minnesota 55435.

Printed in the United States.

Credits
Edited by: Pam Price
Curriculum Coordinator: Nancy Tuminelly
Cover and Interior Design and Production: Mighty Media
Photo Credits: BananaStock Ltd., Comstock, Kelly Doudna, Eyewire Images, John Foxx Images, Hemera, PhotoDisc, Stockbyte

Library of Congress Cataloging-in-Publication Data

Doudna, Kelly, 1963-
      -Ow as in crow / Kelly Doudna.
         p. cm. -- (Word families. Set VII)
      Summary: Introduces, in brief text and illustrations, the use of the letter combination
   "ow" in such words as "crow," "elbow," "mow," and "window."
      ISBN 1-59197-265-5
      1. Readers (Primary) [1. Vocabulary. 2. Reading.] I. Title. II. Series.

   PE1119 .D6845 2003
   428.1--dc21   2002038218

SandCastle™ books are created by a professional team of educators, reading specialists, and content developers around five essential components that include phonemic awareness, phonics, vocabulary, text comprehension, and fluency. All books are written, reviewed, and leveled for guided reading, early intervention reading, and Accelerated Reader® programs and designed for use in shared, guided, and independent reading and writing activities to support a balanced approach to literacy instruction.

Let Us Know

After reading the book, SandCastle would like you to tell us your stories about reading. What is your favorite page? Was there something hard that you needed help with? Share the ups and downs of learning to read. We want to hear from you! To get posted on the ABDO Publishing Company Web site, send us e-mail at:

sandcastle@abdopub.com

SandCastle Level: Transitional

-ow Words

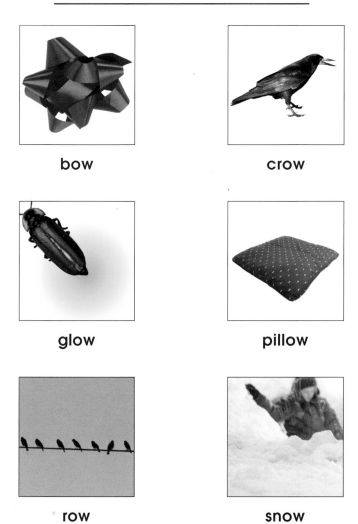

bow

crow

glow

pillow

row

snow

The present has a pink bow.

A crow sits in the tree.

The campfire burns
with an orange glow.

Jo sleeps on a soft
pillow.

The birds sit in a row.

The lanterns glow on the snow.

10

The Slow Crow

The crow
is really slow.

The crow
has time to watch
the garden grow.

The slow crow
finds a hat with a bow.

Now the crow
stops to sit in a row.

The slow crow
feels the breeze blow.

At night the crow
sees a firefly glow.

ZZZZZZZZZ

20

The crow
goes to sleep
on a soft pillow.

The -ow Word Family

blow	mow
bow	pillow
crow	rainbow
elbow	row
flow	show
glow	slow
grow	snow
know	window

Glossary

Some of the words in this list may have more than one meaning. The meaning listed here reflects the way the word is used in the book.

breeze   a wind that blows gently

campfire   a fire lit for warmth and cooking when camping

firefly   a small beetle that glows from the rear part of its body; also called a lightning bug

glow   a steady, low light

lantern   light with a protective cover made from paper, glass, or metal

About SandCastle™

A professional team of educators, reading specialists, and content developers created the SandCastle™ series to support young readers as they develop reading skills and strategies and increase their general knowledge. The SandCastle™ series has four levels that correspond to early literacy development in young children. The levels are provided to help teachers and parents select the appropriate books for young readers.

Emerging Readers
(no flags)

Beginning Readers
(1 flag)

Transitional Readers
(2 flags)

Fluent Readers
(3 flags)

These levels are meant only as a guide. All levels are subject to change.

To see a complete list of SandCastle™ books and other nonfiction titles from ABDO Publishing Company, visit www.abdopub.com or contact us at:

4940 Viking Drive, Edina, Minnesota 55435 • 1-800-800-1312 • fax: 1-952-831-1632